HEINEMANN FIRST ATLAS

Daniel R. Block and Marta Segal Block

Heinemann Library
Chicago, Illinois

Customer Service 888-454-2279
Visit our website at www.heinemannlibrary.com

Designed by Richard Parker and Manhattan Design
Printed and bound in China

11 10 09 08 07
10 9 8 7 6 5 4 3 2 1

Library of Congress Cataloging-in-Publication Data
Block, Daniel, 1967-
    Heinemann first atlas / Daniel R. Block and Marta Segal Block.
    p. cm.
    Includes index.
    ISBN 1-4034-9137-2 (hc)
    1. Children's atlases. 2. Physical geography—Maps for children. I. Block, Marta Segal. II. Title. III. Title: First atlas

    G1021.B5 2006
    912—dc22

                                                           2006042404

Acknowledgments
The author and publishers are grateful to the following for permission to reproduce copyright material: Corbis: p. **5** middle (Connie Ricca), bottom (Carl & Ann Purcell); Getty Images/Taxi p. **5** top; istockphoto p. **4** bottom left; Science Photo Library/NASA/Goddard Space Flight Center p. **4** top right.

Cover photograph of the Earth from space reproduced with permission of Science Photo Library/NASA/Goddard Space Flight Center.

Map illustrations created by International Mapping Associates.

Every effort has been made to contact copyright holders of any material reproduced in this book. Any omissions will be rectified in subsequent printings if notice is given to the publisher.

Contents

What Is a Globe?

A globe is a ball-shaped map.
It looks the way the Earth looks from space.

What Is a Map?

A map is a flat drawing of a part of the Earth. Maps have pictures on them called symbols.

City

River

Mountain

Key

The key on a map explains what the different symbols mean.

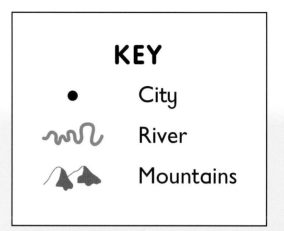

Scale

The scale tells you how far apart things on the map are in real life.

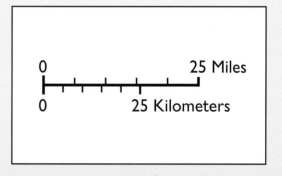

Compass rose

The compass rose shows the directions on a map.

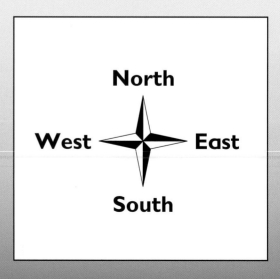

What Are Maps For?

Maps can help you find places.
They can help you find a fire house or a school.

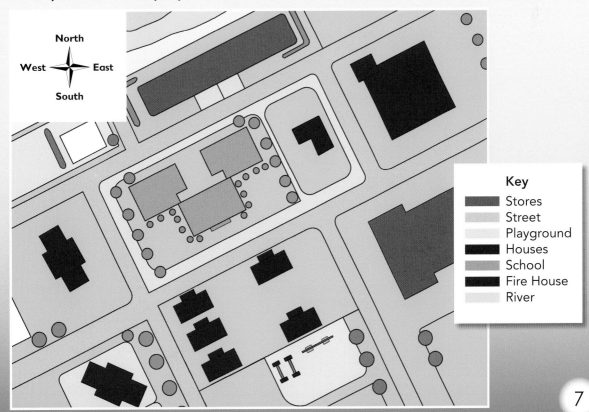

North
West — East
South

Key
Stores
Street
Playground
Houses
School
Fire House
River

The World

This map shows the whole world.
It shows where the seven continents are.

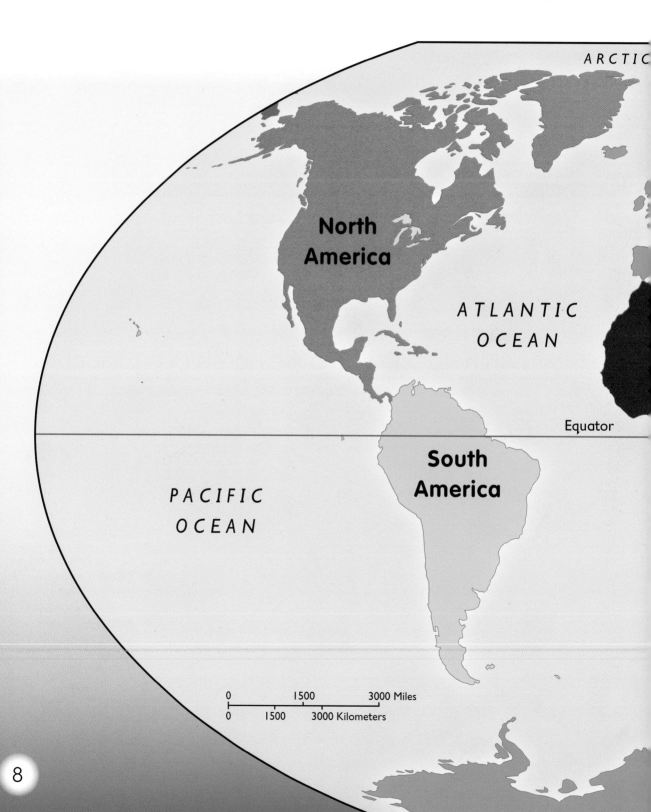

ARCTIC

North
America

ATLANTIC
OCEAN

Equator

South
America

PACIFIC
OCEAN

| 0 | | 1500 | | 3000 Miles |
0   1500   3000 Kilometers

The map also shows the oceans.

OCEAN

Europe

Asia

PACIFIC
OCEAN

Africa

INDIAN
OCEAN

Australia and Oceania

SOUTHERN   OCEAN

Antarctica

Land and Water

Maps can show where mountains and deserts are.

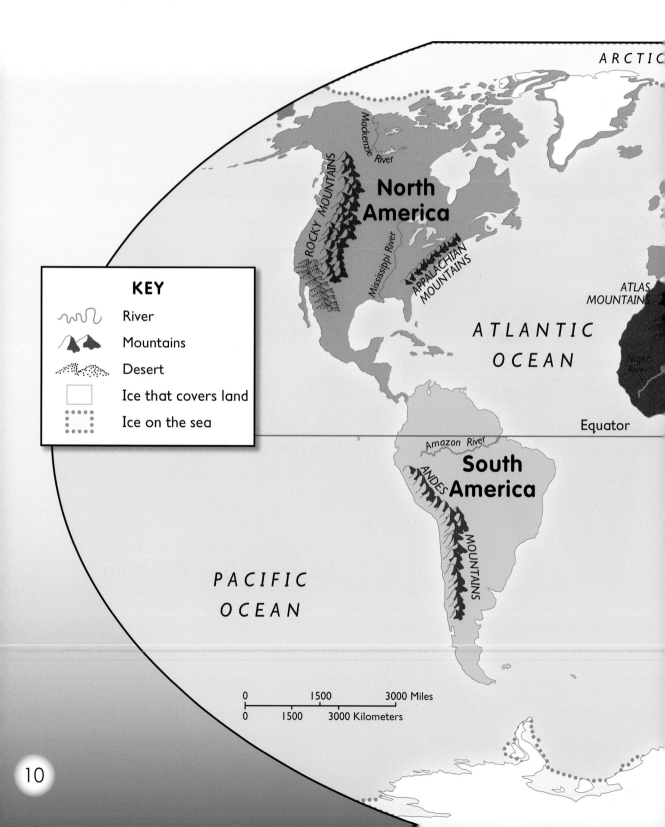

KEY

River
Mountains
Desert
Ice that covers land
Ice on the sea

ARCTIC

Mackenzie River

ROCKY MOUNTAINS

North America

Mississippi River

APPALACHIAN MOUNTAINS

ATLAS MOUNTAINS

ATLANTIC OCEAN

Niger River

Equator

Amazon River

South America

ANDES MOUNTAINS

PACIFIC OCEAN

0   1500   3000 Miles
0   1500   3000 Kilometers

They can show rivers and lakes.

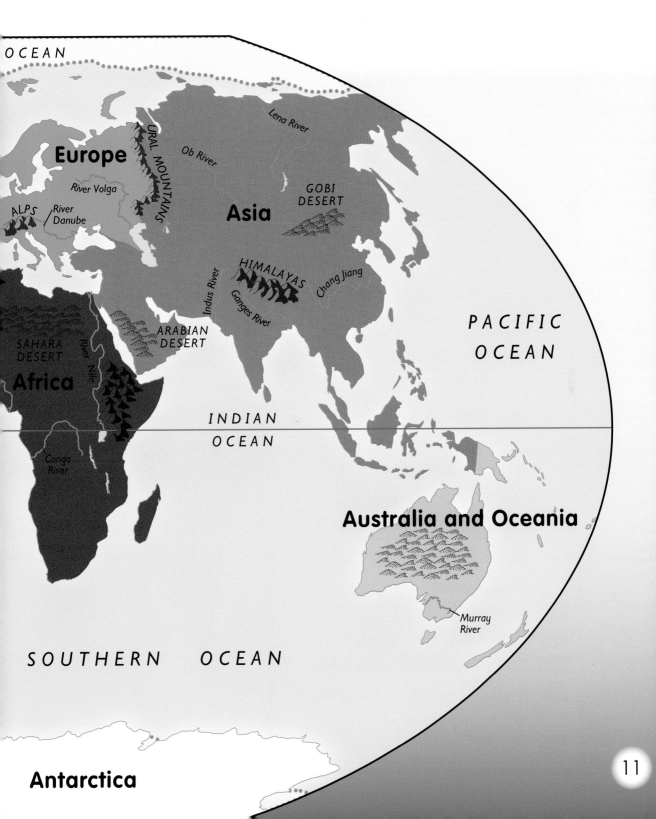

OCEAN

Europe

URAL MOUNTAINS

River Volga

ALPS

River
Danube

SAHARA
DESERT

Africa

River Nile

Congo
River

ARABIAN
DESERT

Indus River

Ganges River

HIMALAYAS

Asia

Ob River

Lena River

GOBI
DESERT

Chang Jiang

INDIAN
OCEAN

PACIFIC

OCEAN

Australia and Oceania

Murray
River

SOUTHERN   OCEAN

Antarctica

Climate

Climate is the usual weather in a place.

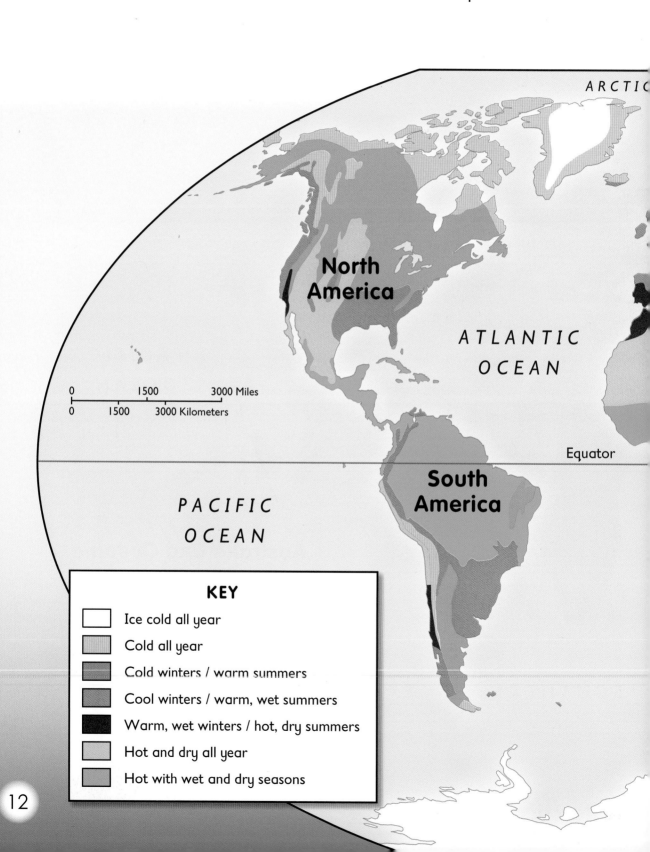

ARCTIC

North America

ATLANTIC OCEAN

0   1500   3000 Miles
0   1500   3000 Kilometers

Equator

South America

PACIFIC OCEAN

KEY

Ice cold all year

Cold all year

Cold winters / warm summers

Cool winters / warm, wet summers

Warm, wet winters / hot, dry summers

Hot and dry all year

Hot with wet and dry seasons

Maps can show what the climate
is like in different parts of the world.

OCEAN

Europe

Asia

Africa

PACIFIC
OCEAN

INDIAN
OCEAN

Australia and Oceania

SOUTHERN   OCEAN

Antarctica

Countries of the World

This map shows some of the countries of the world.

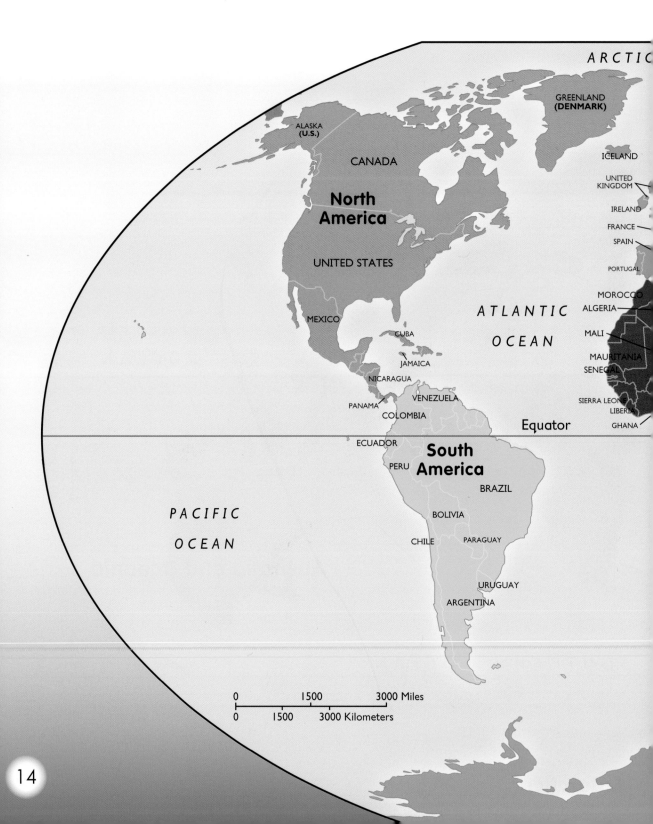

ARCTIC

GREENLAND (DENMARK)

ALASKA (U.S.)

CANADA

ICELAND

UNITED KINGDOM

IRELAND

FRANCE

SPAIN

PORTUGAL

North America

UNITED STATES

MEXICO

MOROCCO

ALGERIA

ATLANTIC

OCEAN

MALI

MAURITANIA

SENEGAL

CUBA

JAMAICA

NICARAGUA

PANAMA

VENEZUELA

COLOMBIA

SIERRA LEONE

LIBERIA

GHANA

Equator

ECUADOR

PERU

South America

BRAZIL

BOLIVIA

PACIFIC

OCEAN

CHILE

PARAGUAY

URUGUAY

ARGENTINA

0	1500	3000 Miles
0	1500	3000 Kilometers

Which continents have a lot of countries?

OCEAN

NORWAY

SWEDEN
FINLAND
ESTONIA
Europe
DENMARK LITHUANIA
POLAND
GERMANY
UKRAINE
AUSTRIA HUNGARY
ROMANIA
ITALY BULGARIA GEORGIA
GREECE TURKEY
TUNISIA
SYRIA
IRAQ
JORDAN IRAN
LIBYA
EGYPT
Africa SAUDI
ARABIA
NIGER OMAN
CHAD
SUDAN
NIGERIA YEMEN
CENTRAL
AFRICAN REP. ETHIOPIA
UGANDA SOMALIA
GABON KENYA
TANZANIA
ANGOLA MOZAMBIQUE
NAMIBIA ZIMBABWE
BOTSWANA MADAGASCAR
SOUTH
AFRICA

RUSSIA

KAZAKHSTAN MONGOLIA
Asia NORTH
KOREA JAPAN
SOUTH
KOREA
CHINA
AFGHANISTAN
NEPAL
PAKISTAN
BANGLADESH
TAIWAN
INDIA
MYANMAR
(BURMA)
THAILAND VIETNAM
CAMBODIA PHILIPPINES
SRI LANKA
MALAYSIA

PACIFIC

OCEAN

INDIAN

OCEAN

INDONESIA PAPUA
NEW GUINEA

AUSTRALIA

Australia and Oceania

NEW
ZEALAND

SOUTHERN   OCEAN

Antarctica

15

The United States

The United States is made up of 50 states.

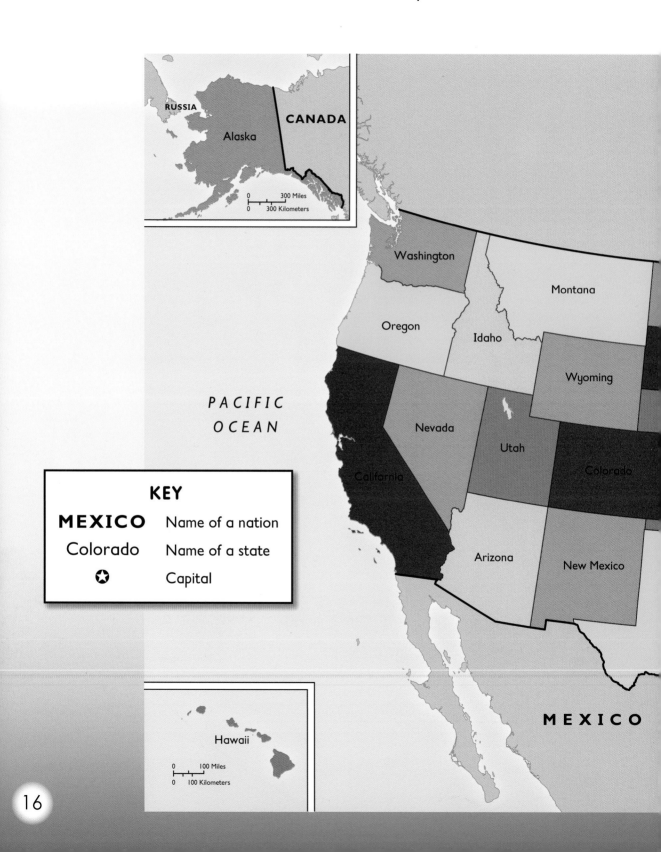

KEY

MEXICO — Name of a nation

Colorado — Name of a state

★ — Capital

It is on the continent of North America.

Rivers and Mountains

This map shows some of the rivers in the United States.

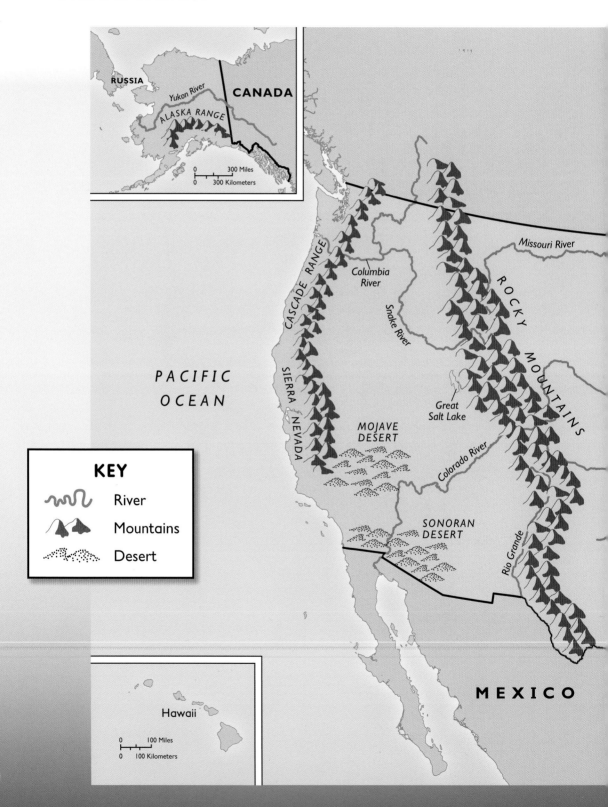

RUSSIA

Yukon River

CANADA

ALASKA RANGE

0   300 Miles

0   300 Kilometers

KEY

River

Mountains

Desert

PACIFIC OCEAN

CASCADE RANGE

SIERRA NEVADA

Columbia River

Snake River

MOJAVE DESERT

SONORAN DESERT

Great Salt Lake

Colorado River

Rio Grande

Missouri River

ROCKY MOUNTAINS

Hawaii

0   100 Miles

0   100 Kilometers

MEXICO

It also shows some of the mountains.

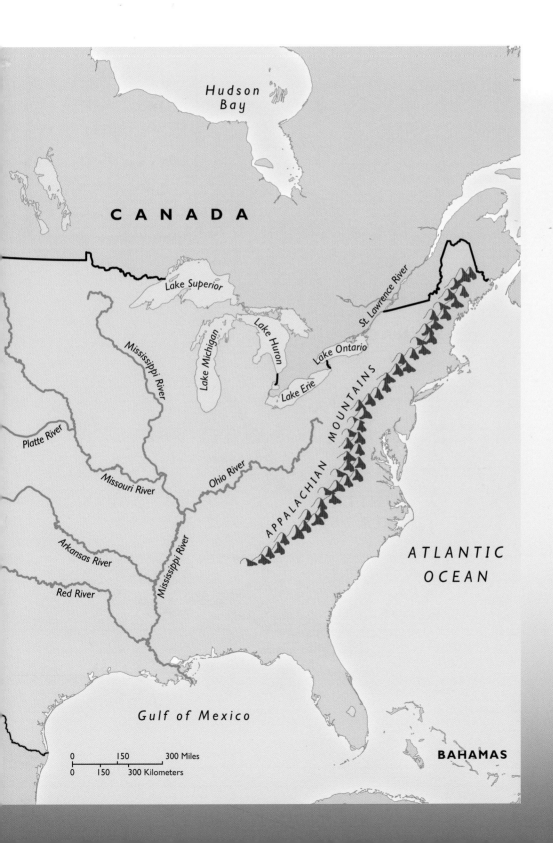

Hudson
Bay

CANADA

Lake Superior

Lake Michigan

Lake Huron

Lake Ontario

Lake Erie

St. Lawrence River

Mississippi River

Platte River

Missouri River

Ohio River

Arkansas River

Mississippi River

Red River

APPALACHIAN MOUNTAINS

ATLANTIC
OCEAN

Gulf of Mexico

BAHAMAS

0   150   300 Miles
0   150   300 Kilometers

North America

North America has some very big countries.
There are also many smaller countries.

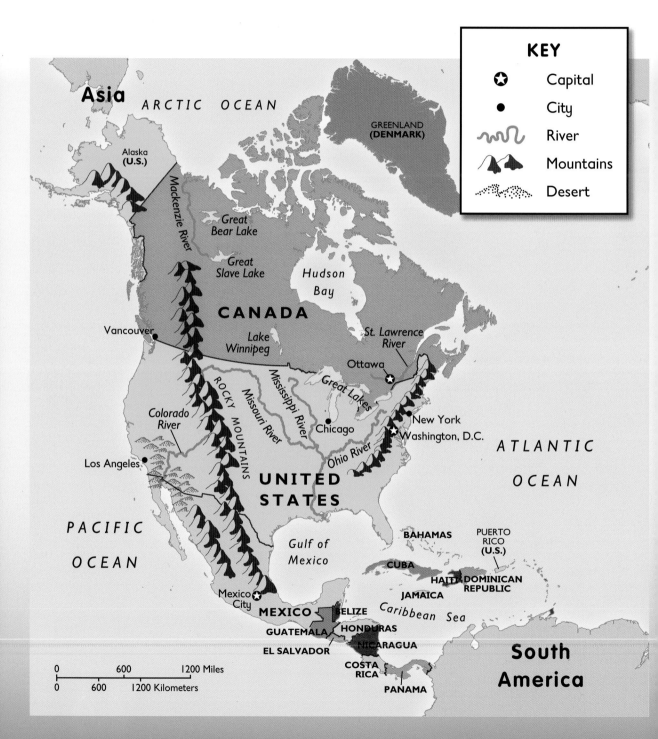

KEY

⭐ Capital
● City
〰 River
⛰ Mountains
⛰ Desert

Asia

ARCTIC OCEAN

GREENLAND
(DENMARK)

Alaska
(U.S.)

Mackenzie River

Great
Bear Lake

Great
Slave Lake

Hudson
Bay

CANADA

Vancouver

Lake
Winnipeg

St. Lawrence
River

Ottawa

Great Lakes

ROCKY MOUNTAINS

Colorado
River

Missouri River

Mississippi River

Chicago

New York

Washington, D.C.

ATLANTIC

OCEAN

Los Angeles

UNITED
STATES

Ohio River

PACIFIC

OCEAN

Gulf of
Mexico

BAHAMAS

PUERTO
RICO
(U.S.)

CUBA

HAITI DOMINICAN
REPUBLIC

JAMAICA

Mexico
City

MEXICO BELIZE

Caribbean Sea

GUATEMALA HONDURAS

EL SALVADOR

NICARAGUA

COSTA
RICA

PANAMA

South
America

0   600   1200 Miles
0   600   1200 Kilometers

South America

The wet Amazon rain forest is in
South America.
So is the dry Atacama Desert.

North
America

Caribbean Sea

Caracas

VENEZUELA

Georgetown
Paramaribo
FRENCH GUIANA
(FRANCE)

Orinoco
River

GUYANA
SURINAME

COLOMBIA

Bogotá

Quito

Equator

ECUADOR

Galápagos
Islands
(ECUADOR)

PERU

Amazon River

ANDES MOUNTAINS

BRAZIL

PACIFIC

OCEAN

Lima

La Paz
BOLIVIA
Sucre

Lake
Titicaca

Brasília

Paraná River

PARAGUAY

Atacama
Desert

0   400   800 Miles

0   400   800 Kilometers

CHILE

ANDES MOUNTAINS

Asunción

Rio de Janeiro
São Paulo

Santiago

URUGUAY
Montevideo

Buenos
Aires

ATLANTIC

OCEAN

ARGENTINA

Falkland Islands
(UNITED KINGDOM)

KEY

☆ Capital

● City

〰 River

⛰ Mountains

Desert

Rain forest

Europe

There are many countries in Europe.

ICELAND

Reykjavik

Norwegian Sea

ATLANTIC OCEAN

NORWAY

SWEDEN

FINLAND

Oslo

Stockholm

Helsinki

ESTONIA

North Sea

UNITED KINGDOM

Dublin

IRELAND

London

DENMARK

Copenhagen

Baltic Sea

Riga

LATVIA

LITHUANIA

Vilnius

RUSSIA

POLAND

BELARUS

NETHERLANDS

Amsterdam

Berlin

Warsaw

Brussels

BELGIUM

GERMANY

Kiev

Paris

LUXEMBOURG

Prague

CZECH REPUBLIC

SLOVAKIA

UKRAINE

Vienna

Budapest

MOLDOVA

SWITZERLAND

AUSTRIA

HUNGARY

FRANCE

SLOVENIA

Milan

ROMANIA

ANDORRA

CROATIA

Belgrade

BOSNIA AND HERZEGOVINA

SERBIA AND MONTENEGRO

PORTUGAL

Barcelona

ITALY

Sarajevo

BULGARIA

Lisbon

Madrid

Rome

Sofia

Istanbul

SPAIN

ALBANIA

MACEDONIA

GREECE

Mediterranean Sea

Athens

Africa

Some are big and some are small.

Africa

Africa is a large continent with many different countries.
The huge Sahara Desert is in Africa.

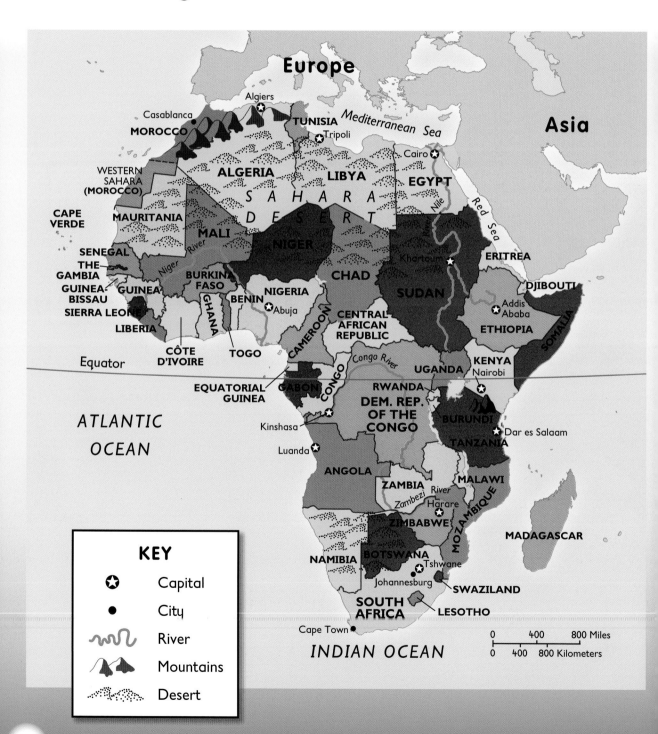

Europe

Asia

Algiers

Casablanca

TUNISIA

Tripoli

Mediterranean Sea

Cairo

MOROCCO

WESTERN
SAHARA
(MOROCCO)

ALGERIA

LIBYA

EGYPT

S A H A R A

Nile

Red Sea

CAPE
VERDE

MAURITANIA

D E S E R T

MALI

River

NIGER

Khartoum

ERITREA

Niger

SENEGAL
THE
GAMBIA
GUINEA-
BISSAU

GUINEA

BURKINA
FASO

CHAD

SUDAN

DJIBOUTI

Addis
Ababa

SIERRA LEONE

GHANA

NIGERIA

BENIN

Abuja

CENTRAL
AFRICAN
REPUBLIC

ETHIOPIA

SOMALIA

LIBERIA

CÔTE
D'IVOIRE

TOGO

CAMEROON

Equator

Congo River

KENYA

UGANDA

Nairobi

EQUATORIAL
GUINEA

GABON

CONGO

RWANDA

ATLANTIC

OCEAN

Kinshasa

DEM. REP.
OF THE
CONGO

BURUNDI

Dar es Salaam

Luanda

TANZANIA

ANGOLA

MALAWI

ZAMBIA

River

Zambezi

Harare

MOZAMBIQUE

ZIMBABWE

MADAGASCAR

NAMIBIA

BOTSWANA

Tshwane

Johannesburg

SWAZILAND

SOUTH
AFRICA

LESOTHO

Cape Town

INDIAN OCEAN

KEY

⭐ Capital

● City

〜 River

⛰ Mountains

⋯ Desert

0   400   800 Miles
0   400   800 Kilometers

Australia and Oceania

Australia is both a continent and a country. Oceania is the area that includes Australia and the islands close to it.

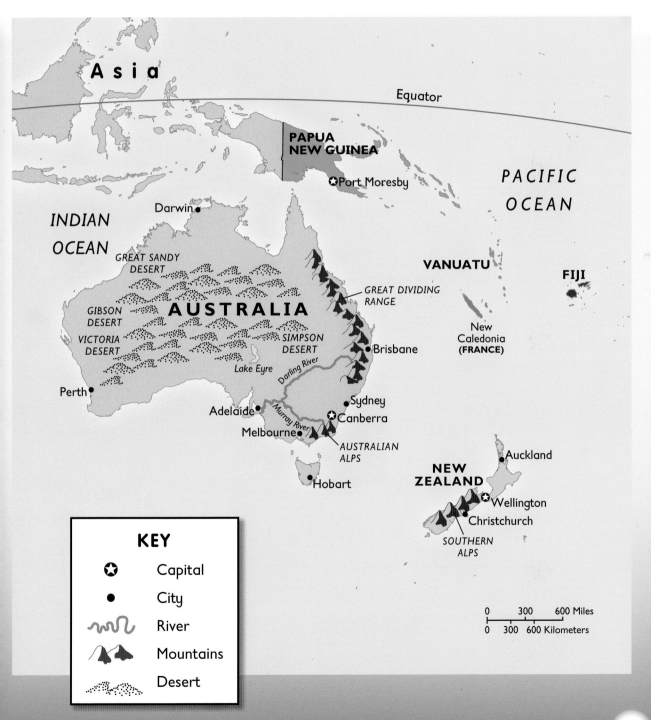

Asia

Equator

PAPUA NEW GUINEA

⭐ Port Moresby

PACIFIC OCEAN

INDIAN OCEAN

Darwin •

GREAT SANDY DESERT

VANUATU

FIJI

GREAT DIVIDING RANGE

GIBSON DESERT

AUSTRALIA

New Caledonia **(FRANCE)**

VICTORIA DESERT

SIMPSON DESERT

• Brisbane

Lake Eyre

Darling River

Perth •

Adelaide •

Murray River

• Sydney
⭐ Canberra

Melbourne •

AUSTRALIAN ALPS

Auckland •

NEW ZEALAND

• Hobart

⭐ Wellington

Christchurch •

SOUTHERN ALPS

KEY

⭐	Capital
•	City
〰	River
⛰	Mountains
⋯	Desert

0	300	600 Miles
0	300	600 Kilometers

Asia

Asia is the largest continent.

More people live in Asia than
on any other continent.

KEY

⭐ Capital

● City

〰️ River

⛰️ Mountains

Desert

Lena River

Lake
Baikal

Ulaanbaatar

MONGOLIA

NORTH
KOREA

Tokyo

Pyongyang

JAPAN

Beijing

Seoul

SOUTH
KOREA

Huang He

Shanghai

CHINA

Chang Jiang

PACIFIC

OCEAN

Mekong River

TAIWAN

MYANMAR
(BURMA)

Hanoi

● Hong Kong

South
China
Sea

Manila

Yangon

LAOS

VIETNAM

PHILIPPINES

THAILAND

Bangkok

CAMBODIA

Phnom
Penh

MALAYSIA

Kuala
Lumpur

SINGAPORE

INDONESIA

Jakarta

The Arctic

The North Pole is covered in ice.
There is no land at the North Pole.

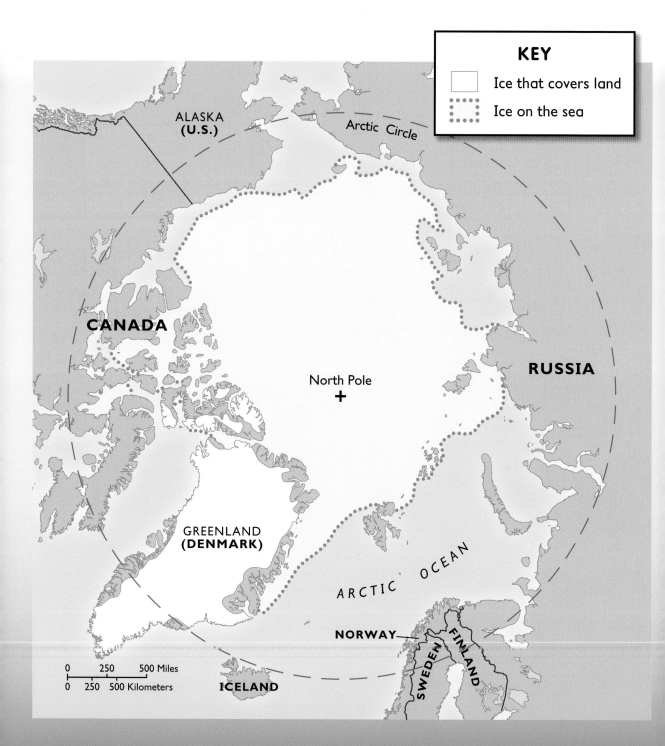

KEY

☐ Ice that covers land

⦙ Ice on the sea

ALASKA (U.S.)

Arctic Circle

CANADA

RUSSIA

North Pole
+

GREENLAND (DENMARK)

ARCTIC OCEAN

NORWAY

SWEDEN

FINLAND

0   250   500 Miles
0   250   500 Kilometers

ICELAND

Antarctica

Antarctica is the coldest continent.
All the land is covered in very thick ice.

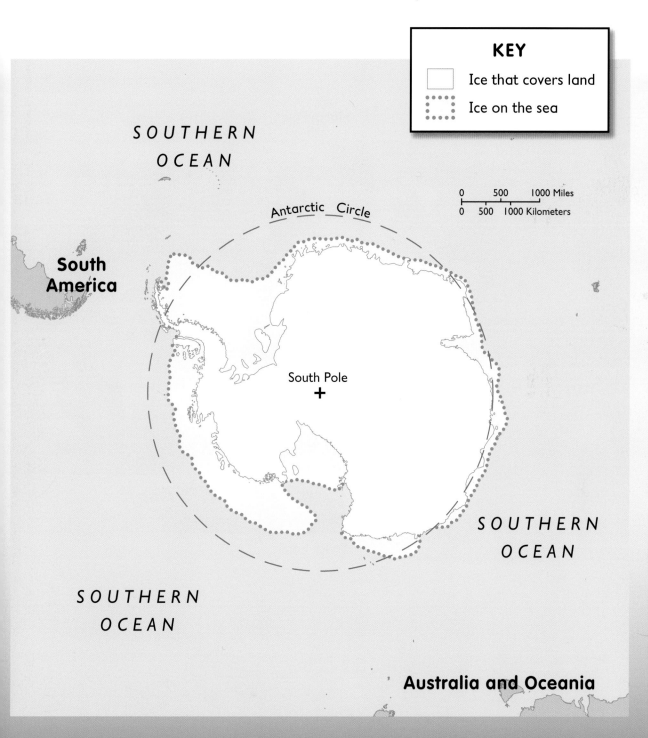

KEY

☐ Ice that covers land

⬚ Ice on the sea

SOUTHERN OCEAN

0   500   1000 Miles
0   500   1000 Kilometers

Antarctic Circle

South America

South Pole
+

SOUTHERN OCEAN

SOUTHERN OCEAN

Australia and Oceania

Lines Around the World

Maps have lines to help show where places are.
The Equator is halfway between the North Pole and the South Pole.

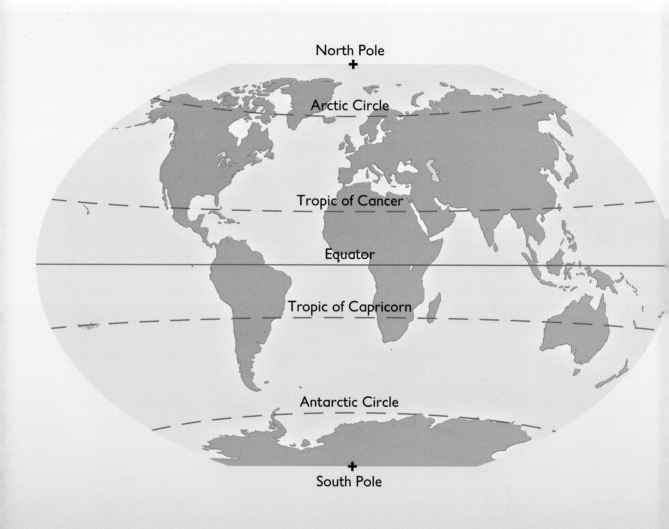

North Pole +

Arctic Circle

Tropic of Cancer

Equator

Tropic of Capricorn

Antarctic Circle

+
South Pole

Glossary

capital

city where the government is located

continent

one of the very large areas of land on the Earth

desert

area of land where it hardly ever rains

North Pole

the point on the Earth that is as far north as you can go

rain forest

thick forest that grows in hot, rainy places

South Pole

the point on the Earth that is as far south as you can go

Index

This is a list of some of the places in this atlas.